TELESEARCH:

Direct Dial the Best Job of Your Life

TELESEARCH:

Direct Dial the Best Job of Your Life

John Truitt

COLLIER BOOKS
Macmillan Publishing Company
New York

This work is most lovingly dedicated
to my beautiful wife, Marisa,
and our little star, Tesia, who helped too,
when she patiently "let Daddy work."

Copyright © 1983 by John F. Truitt

Macmillan Publishing Company
866 Third Avenue, New York, N.Y. 10022
Collier Macmillan Canada, Inc.

Library of Congress Cataloging in Publication Data
Truitt, John.
    Telesearch: direct dial the best job of your life.
    Includes index.
    1. Job hunting. 2. Telephone selling. I. Title.
HF5382.7.T78 1985   650.1'4   84-5878
ISBN 0-02-008850-7 (pbk.)

Macmillan books are available at special discounts
for bulk purchases for sales promotions, premiums,
fund-raising, or educational use. Special editions
or book excerpts can also be created to specifi-
cation. For details, contact:
    Special Sales Director
    Macmillan Publishing Company
    866 Third Avenue
    New York, New York 10022

First Collier Books Edition 1985

10 9 8 7 6 5 4 3 2 1

Telesearch was originally published in a hardcover edition by Facts On File Publications.

Printed in the United States of America

Acknowledgments

This work is a result of my own lifetime experiences and lessons. Many people have contributed to *TELESEARCH* (short for Telephone Job Search) in one way or another. Jim and Rosalie Heacock of The Heacock Literary Agency in Venice, California; Mr. Robert Markel of Wieser & Markel in New York, and Mr. Ed Knappman of Facts On File in New York deserve a lot of the credit. Mr. Sam Weinstein of Venice, California; Mr. Steve Beauchamp of Baton Rouge, Louisiana and Mr. Bob Walker of Houston, Texas helped teach me some of the things I've passed on to my readers. I also learned a great deal from Mr. Ronald R. Byrd and Mr. Terry Roberts of Houston.

Others who have made significant contributions towards helping me reach the point where I could and would share this knowledge are my parents, Mr. and Mrs. Horace Truitt of Madison, Georgia, and my good friend and advisor, the late Mr. Joe Cunningham, also of Madison, Georgia. To all of these people and those good friends and former associates at P. F. Collier, Inc. and Executive Search Consultants, I hereby say, "Thank you," and I hope this work lives up to your expectations.

Special remembrances go to the old Stone Agency in Charleston, South Carolina and to you, too, Funkee, wherever you are. As the Dedication indicates, my wife, Marisa, made the greatest contribution because without her faith and unwavering support, I would never have completed this work.

Thanks,

JOHN TRUITT

Contents

Why TELESEARCH?

Most people resort to one of three methods of job hunting today: they will either try mass-mailing their resumes to as many employers as possible, answering ads in the classifieds, or going through personnel agencies in order to find work. All of these tried and true methods can work, but they are agonizingly slow and offer the very worst chances of success. Why? Because in all three the job seeker plunges into the middle of his crowded competition rather than lifting himself above it or going around it.

If you are to realize the maximum benefit from this text, you must accept this basic principle as fact:

> THE SUCCESS OF ANY JOB SEARCH ULTI-
> MATELY DEPENDS UPON THE QUANTITY AND
> QUALITY OF THE INTERVIEW APPOINTMENTS
> YOU HAVE.... THE MORE YOU HAVE, THE BET-
> TER YOUR CHANCES OF GETTING SERIOUS JOB
> OFFERS.

1

Today the competition for interviews and good career opportunities has become extraordinarily fierce. Unemployment figures are at the highest levels since the Great Depression. As this book goes to press, approximately ten percent of our work force is unemployed. Unemployment percentages may actually be double the national average in many areas of the country, particularly in the northeastern and upper midwestern states.

Rather than trying to discourage or depress you, I am simply pointing out that in many areas of the country you may expect hundreds, if not thousands, of applicants with equal or possibly better qualifications than yours to compete for the same positions that you want. You will have to compete more aggressively and more effectively than others in order to win the kind of interviews and subsequent job offers you deserve.

Sadly enough, most job hunting and career books concentrate upon various styles of resumes and cover letters. They don't teach their readers how to outmaneuver their competition and obtain important interviews during periods of economic recession and high unemployment.

Before writing this book, I did a great deal of research to see if there really was a need for another job hunting book. My determination was reinforced by this startling fact: virtually all of the career books in libraries and book stores today recommend a direct-mail approach to securing interviews. Even the books written by professionals in the personnel business offer no better methods of arranging appointments than by going through an agency (naturally), or sending your resume and cover letter to as many employers as possible with the hope of getting lucky.

The idea of all these "head hunters" writing cover letters and sending out resumes all day is absurd to a professional recruiter. When one earns his money by a contingency fee or on straight commission, he had better have something more reliable than the mail service going for him if he expects to pay the rent on time. The best recruiters and head hunters

2

cannot afford the red tape and delays which are inevitable when dealing with resumes and personnel departments by mail.

Don't Get Stuck In A Stack Of Resumes

If you attempt to use a resume to secure an interview, you will place yourself in a position where you are evaluated for the position before you actually meet anyone from the company. Your writing skills and the information you remembered to include in your resume will be all that a prospective employer will have to evaluate your potential. It is too easy to get turned down without a chance.

While you are waiting for your resume to make it through the mails and proper channels, someone else is being interviewed for the position. You may not realize just how many unsolicited resumes employers and personnel firms receive daily. The large, well-known agencies and corporations receive hundreds of resumes every day from job seekers all over the country. I do not recommend competing against such odds.

Another valid point worth considering if you are presently employed is that confidentiality is not always maintained. You have no way of knowing who might see your resume, nor do you know whether they have friends or relatives who work for your present employer. Search firms and personnel agencies have been sued because one of their client firms was careless with an applicant's resume. For this very reason, many of the more reputable executive search firms have established strict policies against mailing an applicant's resume.

People spend hours, days, sometimes weeks preparing and typing their resumes, sending out mass mailings, and then waiting even longer for replies that, for the most part, never come. They could spend twenty percent of that time contacting prospective employers by phone and get instant results. When one is unemployed and those former paydays

3

keep passing without any paychecks, time really is money!

The telephone is the primary tool of today's professional recruiter. I cannot say why other head hunter-turned-authors do not share this knowledge with their readers. Perhaps they feel that if they divulge all of their secrets they'll no longer be needed.... Who knows?

I do know that any recruiter worth his salt will market his best applicant to twenty or thirty employers in one day by telephone. He will first contact those firms with openings that he knows about, either from his current job orders or from ads placed by the firms in the Sunday classifieds in local newspapers—just like you would. He then gets out his trusty trade directories of companies in his applicant's business and phones the hiring authority listed for each company, giving a brief, enthusiastic presentation of the applicant's personality and qualifications to arrange an interview appointment.

Sure, some recruiters work with resumes but they send a resume to an employer *after contacting them by phone, not before,* as most job hunting books would have you believe. The best of the professional recruiters do not like to send resumes at all. They prefer to rely upon their own salesmanship to persuade an employer to actually meet their applicant rather than review his resume. This is how we will conduct your *TELESEARCH*.

Why Not Go Through An Agency?

After explaining how a good recruiter works, you may wonder why I do not simply advise my readers to work with agencies exclusively. First, examine the difference between employment agencies, personnel firms, executive search consultants, career counselors, and the rest. All may be divided into two basic categories: company-paid and applicant-paid.

Executive search consultants (head hunters), employer-paid personnel and recruiting firms all work for the employers. Their primary function is to find candidates who are suited to fill the job orders they receive from companies that have agreed to pay a fee for their services. Applicant-paid agencies spend their time finding jobs for their applicants. It is primarily a question of loyalties and paying the piper.

All The Sharks In The Pool

If you are having a tough time finding work, an employer-paid recruiting firm will not do you much good. Professional recruiters are taught (as well they should be) to spend their time working with their "value job orders" and "value applicants." We are not concerned with job orders, but a "value applicant" is commonly defined as one who is marketable, in demand, open to salary, cooperative, and has some other qualities that make him or her more sought after than anyone else in the recruiter's files. Today's smart professional recruiter spends his time working only with "winners." Recruiters and head hunters are not known for their charity, nor will they ever be. Most (the best) work on a straight commission basis and cannot afford to spend their precious time betting on "possibilities."

I've never cared for such an attitude, but being a professional recruiter myself, I discovered that my banker, mortgage holder, and other creditors seemed to be in absolute agreement with this philosophy. Remember:

> IF YOU ARE A "VALUE APPLICANT," THE EMPLOYER-PAID RECRUITER MAY NEED YOU MORE THAN YOU NEED HIM. IF NOT, YOU MAY NEED HIM BUT HE CANNOT AFFORD TO TRY TO HELP YOU.

Here is where the applicant-paid employment counselor comes to the rescue. Ah, but there is a catch.... If you use one of these agencies, it will cost you several thousand dollars. If you are unhappy with the position after you have started, you will still have to pay the fee, unless, of course, you are fired by the employer within the "guarantee period." It's a dilemma, isn't it?

Consider, if you will, the career "strategists" or counseling firms who will charge several thousand dollars to "evaluate" and "design" your career path, write your resume, coach your interview skills, and send you on your way with a lighter wallet but without a single interview, much less a job. They enjoy feeding upon the middle-aged executive who has begun to wonder if he would not be happier running a fishing yacht in the Bahamas or a hunting lodge in the Grand Tetons.

The last of these services has the smallest bite but may offer the most catastrophic results to the job seeker. Many resume services offer their best product as a bound, typeset, embossed-on-parchment masterpiece of literary excellence that costs "only a couple of hundred dollars" and is guaranteed to end up in any self-respecting hiring authority's wastebasket. The problem here is that resume services charge by the page—the larger the resume, the bigger the sale and the better the profit for them. They may also recommend cover pictures, the most expensive paper, high-temperature printing, and costly bindings. Most hiring authorities take a sour view of all these expensive trappings.

THE MORE EXPENSIVE THE RESUME, THE MORE DISAPPOINTING THE APPLICANT.

If you are becoming somewhat leery of what may seem like a school of sharks feeding upon the nation's job market, I will not fault your judgment.

Before I am assailed by my former colleagues, let me hasten to say that there are many highly ethical professionals engaged in all of the above-mentioned endeavors. I do think, however, that you should be aware of some of the motives that may influence the statements and suggestions made in their sales propaganda.

Fee-Paid Recruiters

Although no recruiter will be able to devote his full time to any single applicant's case, anyone making a serious effort at finding a career position should at least register with one or two reputable, employer-paid recruiting or personnel firms. If a position opens for which you are qualified, a recruiter cannot help you if he does not know about you. Should a head hunter ever contact you about an opportunity, by all means meet with him and hear the details. Opportunity knocks only so often during your career.

A good recruiter can be invaluable in presenting your skills, negotiating salary, bonuses, reviews, seniority for benefits, and vacation time while pushing to close the placement and move the company off its rear to make the offer. A voice whispering good things about you in the employer's ear cannot hurt your case. A good recruiter can greatly assist you in getting exactly what you want from an employer if you are cooperative and truthful with him.

Choose only employer-paid recruiters and counselors who are known for their successful efforts with companies and applicants in your line of work. The finest sales recruiter in the country will not be able to provide much assistance to an accountant, factory worker, or chemist. The easiest way of recruiting a recruiter is by asking your former supervisor or any hiring authority in your industry which agencies and recruiters they deal with most often. Friends and co-workers may also be able to recommend a good counselor. Those agencies that repeatedly advertise for professionals in your field should be worth investigating as well. You can always look the recruiter in the eye and ask if he has had much success placing people with a similar background to yours.

Do not expect much activity, but if the recruiter you have chosen is any good and you are marketable, he should have arranged several interviews within ten days. If he hasn't, and you are still inclined to seek professional assistance, try another. Once you feel you have found a good recruiter and he is arranging meaningful interviews for you, give him your full cooperation. After all, the employer will pay the fee, so everything the recruiter does is free to you. Do not waste his time or yours. The higher salary the recruiter can negotiate for you, the higher his fee. In this sense, at least he is on your side.

Applicant-Paid Agencies

You will not need to pay an agency to find a job for you if you can understand the information in this book and muster enough self-discipline to follow the instructions it contains. If, however, after practicing the guidelines persistently, you continue to fail, go ahead and seek professional help. A few thousand dollars is a lot of money, but it may not be too much to pay if it is the only way you can secure desirable employment.

The applicant-paid agency should be chosen with the same criterion as the employer-paid counselor: a reputation for successful placements in your field. Carefully read any contracts or agreements you are asked to sign and choose a counselor who seems sincere about helping you. Be frank with your counselor and consider, cautiously, each offer you receive through him. You should not allow a counselor to pressure you into accepting an offer unless you believe it is the kind of position you will be happy with. You certainly do not want to pay several thousand dollars for a job and then find that you do not like it. When you are paying the fee you have every right to expect fast action, or find another agency.

Other Third Parties

Local, state, and federal employment offices, public job assistance programs, agencies, non-profit organizations like

Forty-Plus, and the various alumni placement offices can offer valuable assistance in locating openings. Make sure you are given time to prepare for interviews arranged by such offices. These organizations, though they mean well, seem to enjoy sending applicants over for an interview appointment the same day it is arranged.

Resume services are useful if you cannot type or find it impossible to write your own resume. We'll discuss resumes in Chapter Five. If you ask a service to prepare your resume, make them work for their money by insisting upon a one-page resume on plain white paper. Avoid any "deluxe" styles.

Mailing lists are a waste of money. If the hiring authorities listed for the targeted companies are still employed with those firms, you may rest assured that by now they have come up with methods of shielding themselves from the rising sea of faceless resumes currently flooding their offices. Mailing lists of executive search firms and employment agencies are truly pointless because unsolicited resumes are seldom even read by anyone other than a secretary or file clerk. Recruiters like to find their own candidates and abhor going through stacks of unsolicited resumes.

A good psychiatrist or psychologist would probably do you more good than a career strategist or counselor if you are truly depressed, confused about your career goals, or just can't seem to get it together. Believe it or not, you may save thousands of dollars in fees too. Once you know what you want, this book will help you find it.

An Important Decision

Should you elect to use a recruiter or personnel consultant, bear in mind:

COUNSELORS AND RECRUITERS CANNOT CONTACT ANY COMPANIES YOU HAVE ALREADY CONTACTED ON YOUR OWN.

9

You must tell your counselor whom you have contacted or you may be embarrassed when an employer who has been considering you for a position informs you that several recruiters contacted him about you in one week! It could damage your chances of being offered the position. An employer may think you are so desperate that you've contacted every agency in town. He may even question your integrity.

Forget Others; Rely On Yourself

When considering the pros and cons of using an agency or conducting your own job search, take a hard look at the odds for success. During periods of extremely high unemployment, recruiters, agencies, and other personnel firms as well as public employment offices are literally swamped with requests for assistance. These people are human and can do only so much for each individual. If they begin marketing one applicant to employers and run into a negative response, they will simply lay that file aside and begin marketing another applicant. In fact, you will have to stand pretty tall in their eyes to begin with if you are to receive any attention at all. Why throw yourself into the middle of the herd? Why turn over complete control of your career destiny to a stranger whom you have probably met briefly, only once?

If your pro football team was in the Super Bowl and you needed to move the ball only two yards for the winning touchdown in the final seconds of the game, would you let one of the fans carry the ball? No, you would more likely ask your best running back—someone who has performed consistently well for you all season—to take the ball in for the score.

When it comes to the career game, you are the best ball carrier on your team. You can give your job search a full-time and much more sincere effort because it is your paycheck, career, and future at stake. In the next chapters, you will learn the secrets of *TELESEARCH*, the same basic procedure a counselor or recruiter would follow in order to market you to as many prospective employers as possible in the shortest period of time.

ALL OF YOUR PAYCHECKS FOR THE FOLLOW-
ING YEAR MAY WELL DEPEND UPON YOUR ABIL-
ITY TO OUTMANEUVER AND "OUT-INTERVIEW"
THE COMPETITION.

TELESEARCH is like a straight line. It is the shortest route between you and the career position you really want. You will learn to outmaneuver the crowd and avoid long lines and red tape while finding opportunities quickly, even when few are listed. With *TELESEARCH*, you may reasonably expect to have a good job within a week or two. Third parties and the other schemes (especially mass mailing resumes) will take at least a month or two to get results, if not much longer. With *TELESEARCH* you will not spend weeks or months waiting for a response and you will not wonder whether your resume reached the right person.

You will have direct contact and immediate dialogue with the hiring authority instead of being screened by the personnel department or an agency. You will not be just another faceless resume. Employers receive tons of resumes but remarkably few phone calls from applicants themselves.

TELESEARCH is cheaper, too. Fees, lists, mass mailings, printing, and postage can be very costly. All you need for *TELESEARCH* is a telephone—and there are also ways of saving on long-distance calls.

If you control your own job search, you will have more opportunities to sell yourself and your background firsthand to the hiring authority. This greatly improves your chances of actually getting meaningful interview appointments. Can't you be persuasive when you really want to be?

Those who would follow the simple guidelines in this book should find themselves in the hiring authority's office interviewing for the position while their competitors are sitting in personnel agency waiting rooms or at home stuffing envelopes.

There are two more definite advantages to marketing yourself rather than having a third party do it:

First, you know your schedule and may arrange an appointment on the spot. Valuable time may be lost if a counselor has to make several calls back and forth just to confirm an appointment for an interview.

The second, and possibly greatest, advantage is that if you arrange your own interview and the employer is seriously considering you for the position, it will not cost his company several thousand dollars in agency fees to hire you. He may even be able to offer you more money if he is not required to pay an agency's fee. The employer could offer you the position over a more qualified candidate, submitted by a recruiter, simply to save the fee and keep those funds in his operating budget. It happens quite frequently.

During peak periods of economic growth and expansion, only a very small percentage of all job openings are filled by head hunters, recruiting firms, personnel agencies, and employment agencies combined. This small percentage shrinks considerably during periods of deep recession. As unemployment figures rise, even fewer companies will need the recruiters' help with so much talent available "on the streets."

The bottom line as to whether you should use third parties or not really boils down to this:

NO ONE WILL CARE AS MUCH ABOUT YOUR JOB SEARCH AS YOU. NO ONE ELSE WILL WORK AS HARD AS YOU TO FIND THE "RIGHT JOB."

You Can Do It!

TELESEARCH is not impossible nor even that difficult to learn. I have heard others say that most people are afraid to sell themselves over the telephone or that many of us have a "phone phobia," a fear of using the telephone. Many people have a fear of water until they learn to swim. Is it actually fear or lack of know-how? If you know whom to call, when to call, what to say, and how to say it, you may find *TELE-SEARCH* just as pleasant as a cool dip on a hot summer day— although far more rewarding. This book will teach you all of these things and more.

In the following pages, I will share with you the sum of my fifteen years of experience in interviewing thousands of job hunters from all walks of life. You will learn to "prep" yourself for interviews, just as I would prepare you to interview for a career position with one of my client firms.

Your main objective will be to master all the secrets and techniques of overcoming the competition and getting serious offers, quickly.

> YOUR GOAL IN EACH INTERVIEW HAS TO BE
> TO SECURE AN *OFFER*. WITHOUT A SOLID OF-
> FER, YOU HAVE NOTHING; NO OPPORTUNITY
> NOR SALARY TO CONSIDER, NO TITLE, NO BEN-
> EFITS...NOTHING.

You will never even hear the full story from an employer until he extends to you a formal offer. This is why we seek out and interview with companies in the first place.

Regardless of your education, experience, income, age, race, sex, nationality, or employment status, this book is for you. Prepare yourself to be on a full offensive until you have a solid offer. An all-out offensive like this will require a full-time effort on your part, but it should not take too long to complete your job search successfully—if you follow these instructions as closely as you can.

The greatest saving aspect of our nation's overstuffed job market is the fact that all of the interviewers and employers we come in contact with are still human beings, just like you and me.

IF YOU CAN MAKE THEM WANT YOU, THEY
WILL DO THEIR BEST TO SEE THAT *YOU* ARE
HIRED RATHER THAN SOMEONE ELSE.

We have all been taught what the best candidate for employment in our own individual profession is supposed to
look and act like. In this book, you will learn to look and act
better than any other candidate the employer is likely to
interview for the same position. If you decide now to apply
yourself and concentrate upon outperforming the competition before, during, and after the interview, the employer
will want to offer you the opportunity.

Discrimination And Other Problems

Although age, sex, and racial discrimination are almost history in many large corporations, these problems still persist.
I am ashamed to say they are even more widespread among
my colleagues in small business. Small firms whose policies
are primarily formulated by one individual fall victim to the
prejudice and preconceptions of that person. They are too
small in most cases to be noticed by the Equal Employment
Opportunity Commission (EEOC).

NEITHER YOU NOR YOUR INTERVIEWER WILL
CHANGE COMPANY POLICY DURING YOUR
FIRST INTERVIEW.

Moreover, if the employer has any inkling that you might
be some kind of activist, you can forget about working for
that firm. Right or wrong, that is the way things are.
Consequently, I will not discuss your rights or freedom of
information laws, nor shall I guide you to the EEOC if you
feel your rights have been infringed upon. If so inclined,
you may handle that yourself. Besides, the way to overcome
discrimination is not by jamming yourself down some em-

14

ployer's throat but by being the kind of person he wants to hire regardless of your age, race, or sex.

WHEN THE GOING GETS TOUGH, THE TOUGH GET GOING!

This old slogan from my days in direct sales seems appropriate here. If you know you will face prejudice or other problems in your job search due to your lack of experience or formal education, too many jobs in your past, or too many lay-offs in your field—then you must also realize that you will have to work harder than others to overcome these negatives. You will need to locate more opportunities, arrange more interviews, and interview more aggressively and more impressively than others in order to find a worthwhile career position.

As more and more women, minorities, and older adults contribute to increased sales, profits, and major technical breakthroughs in their companies, prejudice in business will pass.

Why I Wrote This Book

Earlier, you will recall, I stated that head hunters were not a very charitable breed. This is primarily due to our desire to manage our time effectively rather than to a lack of compassion. Most of us would not be involved in the human resource field if we did not like people or care about their problems.

As a recruiter, I was constantly faced with people who needed help but for whom I knew that none of my clients would pay a hiring fee. Most frustrating to me was the knowledge that I could teach these people, whom I liked and admired, how to help themselves if I could just spend a couple of hours with each of them. Writing this book is my way of doing that.

You don't have to be unemployed. You need not keep working at a job that you despise, nor must you remain with an employer who does not appreciate you or cannot afford your services. Regardless of economic conditions, this book will teach you how to change jobs, now. In fact, after reading it, you may literally pick up your telephone and change your life for the better.

2

Your TELESEARCH Plan

Begin by looking ahead. Decide now to put behind you for good the events and circumstances that have led to your present situation. To be successful, you will need all of your powers of concentration for the voyage ahead.

You cannot change your past, anyway. Your work history, education, skills, and experience are as much a part of you as your name. The manner in which you capitalize upon your experience, target your prospective market, and then present yourself to that market will ultimately determine your degree of success. Before we can put your *TELESEARCH* plan to work, we should look at some of the broader options available to you.

New Career Or New Employer?

As tempting as it may seem in depressed times, you should never consider changing fields unless you really despise your work or have reached the end of your rope.

You are, effectively, starting over again when you change fields completely. All of your years of experience and training will be worthless. You will be a "trainee" again. You and your family may not be able to afford the substantial loss in income that you can expect from a trainee's salary. Employers are not at fault. No trainee is worth the same salary as an experienced employee.

There are literally thousands more trainees out there seeking employment than professionals with your particular experience and expertise. In areas of the country with the highest levels of unemployment, competition for trainee-type openings could be overwhelming. If you are already unemployed, the only selling points you will be able to muster in the interviews are your maturity, intelligence, and willingness to work hard and learn a new profession. With the possible exception of maturity, these other points are the same qualities that all trainees have to sell. Usually, employers prefer to hire younger people as trainees because of the lower pay. Often, those who attempt a change in career fields end up learning the meaning of the term "overqualified" the hard way.

Think again. It might be better to plan a major change in careers when you are employed and have time to study, prepare, and save enough money to get you and your family through the training period. Professionally, this is the best advice I can offer.

We all know there are exceptions. I am one of them. If I had not moved from sales management to executive search years ago, you would not be reading this book now. That change in careers cost me almost *half* my annual income the first year, but it was well worth the sacrifice in the long run. There are times when we are so underchallenged, underpaid, or underappreciated in our present line of work that we are willing to sacrifice anything to get out. If this describes your present situation and you can afford the sacrifice, then by all means, start planning to change fields today!

Strategy For Changing Fields

The amount of your earnings that you may expect to sacrifice by changing career fields can be held to a minimum if you utilize as much of your previous experience as possible when planning your strategy.

THE MORE YOU CAN RELATE YOUR PREVIOUS EXPERIENCE TO THE POSITION YOU WANT, THE MORE YOU WILL BE WORTH TO YOUR NEW EMPLOYER.

For example, imagine that an accountant for a ball-bearing manufacturer wants to become a salesperson. The best means of maximizing her years of experience might be to sell accounting services to manufacturing firms. She might sell inventory or credit services; computers; time-sharing; office systems, machines, and supplies; or even ball-bearings. If she attempted to capitalize upon her experience this way, she might have to learn only one thing...how to sell.

A 180-degree turn in careers may actually require two 90-degree turns. If the career you've been eyeing seems closed to trainees, plan to work in a similar industry to gain experience before making the big move. If you will need additional formal education or training, you might give serious thought to taking a part-time job or another position in your present career field to support yourself while seeking a full-time position in the field of your choice. This would also be good advice if a particularly long job search is anticipated.

If you have a strong desire to enter a particular profession, try to associate with those already employed in that field.

Some of them may introduce you to the "right people" who could give you a start. The numerous professional trade associations, your local Chamber of Commerce, and your own personal contacts may offer worthwhile assistance.

Your present employer's customers as well as her suppliers will recognize your skill, speak your language, and may offer you an opportunity to work in a new field while still getting paid for the experience you already have.

Where The Money Is

THE HIGHEST SALARY INCREASES USUALLY OCCUR WHEN ONE GOES TO WORK FOR HIS PRESENT OR LAST EMPLOYER'S DIRECT COMPETITOR.

I realize that many companies would have us believe they will not hire from a competitor. I would be unemployed, myself, if this were true. Most employers I know love to boast about stealing a star performer from their archrival. They will pay dearly for the one they really want, too.

If you are bored or need more challenge and responsibility, do not overlook the possibility of solving your problems by seeking a promotion with your present employer (if you are still employed) or moving to a higher position with a competitor before making up your mind to discard most of your professional training by changing fields. A new environment, new people, higher salary, and a fresh, new set of challenges and responsibilities may quench your thirst for change. Give it a shot. If it does not work out, then start looking for a new career.

Large Or Small Vessel?

Another way of getting out of a "rut" is by moving from a large corporation to a small competitor or vice versa. The two are entirely different. Comparing the advantages and disadvantages of each requires a long inward look at the type of career opportunity, work environment, responsibility, salary, and benefits that you will need. I say look inward because what may appear to be a distinct disadvantage to one individual might seem like a golden opportunity to another. Personally, I am an entrepreneur. I naturally favor smaller companies, so I'll discuss them first.

Speed & Maneuverability

Small companies, as a rule, really do pay better than large corporations. There are several reasons for this.

Small companies need your valuable experience more than large firms because they have neither extensive training facilities of their own nor a huge pool of employees from which they can find and promote managers. Successful small firms often grow so fast that they may not have had time to develop the departments their new size demands, much less the managers to run them. So, they steal promising talent from their larger competitors by offering higher salaries, bonuses, impressive titles, and sometimes even a piece of the action in the form of stock or an eventual partnership. This is possible due to lower overhead, a higher return on investment (ROI), and fewer executives and stockholders to split up the pie. Fewer "perks" and benefits (usually true in smaller firms) also leave more money for salaries.

Personally, I enjoy the informality and individuality of other employees, the freedom of expression, camaraderie, team spirit, and even the belt-tightening all must occasionally endure together to build a small business into a successful enterprise. You can really see your own contribution to the growth and success of your small company. These things may not always show up on your paycheck, but they can make a difference in the attitude you have about going to work in the morning.

The Fast Track

A tiger shark receives far greater attention in a small lagoon than in the Pacific. You may see more potential for personal advancement in a small company if you consider yourself a "fast-tracker" and are hungry for challenges, recognition, promotions, and greater responsibilities and rewards.

Chances are, if you work late on a project at your small firm, the only other employee in the office that late will be the president or owner of the company. He or she will not forget your extra efforts.

Red tape should be almost nonexistent in the small company, so your ideas and input will be more likely to reach senior management in one piece. You should have a better chance of getting the credit, too. Even today, in many small companies one may still walk into the boss's office, describe a job that needs doing, profess the willingness to direct the project, and get a promotion on the spot!

Those who seem to advance more rapidly than others usually begin their careers with a large corporation (often recruited prior to graduation from school) and stay with them from two to four years, taking advantage of superior training and learning their industry while being groomed for management. They then switch to a small competitor for a few years, where they raise their title and salary. Next they return to a large company as a full-blown executive earning a much greater salary than if they had stayed with their first large firm for the long haul. They may switch back and forth several times during their career as they work their way to the top of their field. Some people might question their company loyalty or accuse these fast-trackers of job-hopping, but it does seem to be the quickest route to success.

Possible Problems With The Small Firm

While there are drawbacks to working for a small firm, the most serious questions that must be answered to your satisfaction will have to do with the owner(s) and/or the company's financial condition.

Entrepreneurs are known as imaginative and hard-working as well as stubborn and individualistic. They can often appear absent-minded. While everyone else is toasting the office manager's birthday after work, the entrepreneur's mind may be on shipping dates or deadlines yet to be met. Her business occupies her mind during most of her waking hours. Entrepreneurs are a wild and wonderful breed, so be prepared for anything!

Entrepreneurs do not always make the best employers. They often cannot understand why employees will not work as hard as they will and seem to have an inherent reluctance to delegate authority. If you seek a management position with a small firm, pay particular attention to laying the ground rules for your authority and the freedom of decision you will have. The entrepreneur's reluctance or inability to delegate is often misconstrued as an ego problem. Entrepreneurs definitely have a healthy opinion of themselves (often well-earned). The entrepreneur's problem in delegating usually stems from the fact that when she started the business, she probably did almost everything herself and developed her own way of doing things. Many times it is easier for her to step in and handle a job herself than go through her own channels. This can be very frustrating to the new manager fresh from a large company, where she became accustomed to channels, departmentalization, and a large support staff. In the smallest of firms, policies may actually fluctuate with the mood of the owner.

Once you have decided you can live with the boss, you may wish to check into the company's financial condition. If you are still employed, you can run a D&B (Dun & Bradstreet) report through your present employer's membership. A friendly banker or broker might do this for you. Your banker may know a great deal about the firm you are investigating or should be willing to help you find out more about a prospective employer's reputation and financial condition as a service to you, the bank's customer.

23

It may be difficult to gather information about a privately held company's financial condition, but a few hours on the telephone with the company's customers, suppliers, competitors, and your local Chamber of Commerce or Better Business Bureau should give you a pretty good picture of their reputation and professional standing in the community. Evaluating the owners and financial condition of a small firm usually sifts down to your own "gut feelings." Try to conduct as much research as you can but pay attention to these instincts. You will be correct in your judgment more often than not.

Recent graduates will not find a small firm's inadequate or nonexistent training program very helpful to their careers. Older equipment, "bare-bones" benefits, the lack of tuition refund plans (company-paid continuing education programs), and less security (small firms cannot always carry large payrolls during slow market conditions) are all negatives that you should consider. That team spirit we all enjoy in the small company may be lost forever if it is acquired by a large conglomerate. There have been quite a lot of these acquisitions recently.

Solid & Seaworthy

Often, the shortcomings of the small company are the same areas where large corporations excel. Whenever possible, fresh graduates should make every effort to begin their professional careers in large, well-known corporations. They will receive modern, extensive training and indoctrination into corporate life. Students should apply during campus recruiting drives in hopes of being recruited by one of the larger firms. They will begin their careers with a solid foundation that cannot be matched by a small business. Also, spending the first two to four years of your career with a brand name company looks impressive on your resume.

Many large companies have benefit booklets that are thicker

than their annual reports. You may expect hospitalization, maternity, dental, life, and other attractive insurance plans for your entire family. Retirement plans, sick leave, tuition refund, profit sharing, paid vacations, and paid holidays are standard in most large firms. Many now offer lavish relocation packages and company-assisted mortgage loans to soften transfers. Van-pooling, car-sharing, flexible hours, day-care centers, and even company spas and exercise rooms have lately become more commonplace. Many of the largest corporations have special personnel assistants or arrangements with private consultants to help employees who have been laid off find employment elsewhere. This is called "outplacement assistance." Significant bonuses and stock options are normally reserved for senior management in the large companies.

Many employees enjoy greater job security with a large firm, although, as recently demonstrated, none of them is entirely recession-proof. Your duties and responsibilities should be more clearly defined in a larger organization because there are more employees to handle the work load. There is a better chance of transferring to a different department if you become bored with your work or have problems with a particular supervisor or another employee. Finally, in a large corporation you will be exposed to the most modern, advanced methods, systems, and equipment available to business. Your familiarity and expertise with modern equipment will be a valuable selling point with your next employer should you ever decide to change jobs.

Weighing The Differences

You must decide for yourself which size organization is best for you. Moving from a large firm to a small one could be your biggest promotion ever. If you are presently employed by a large firm, you may sacrifice benefits by going to work for a small company but you will make it up in cash and rapid advancement. During periods of high unemployment, you may find a position faster with a small firm because there are more small firms around. If you are with a small company now, this may be your chance to have a large firm pay you a greater salary than you are earning plus all those benefits.

Whatever your inclination, either choice has merit. Base your decision upon whichever work environment seems to suit your personality and career goals best.

Career Sense

"TIMING YOUR MOVE FOR MAXIMUM SALARY GAIN" MEANS LOOKING FOR A NEW OPPORTUNITY WHILE YOU STILL HOLD YOUR PRESENT POSITION.

If you are now unemployed, you already know the wisdom of this advice. Here is a word to those who may still be employed but remain unconvinced:

IF YOU QUIT YOUR PRESENT POSITION BEFORE FINDING A NEW ONE, IT WILL COST YOU *AT LEAST TEN PERCENT OF YOUR TOTAL ANNUAL INCOME,* NOT TO MENTION THE PAYCHECKS LOST WHILE YOU ARE UNEMPLOYED.

Prospective employers will seldom offer an increase in salary to someone who is unemployed. They will feel justified in offering you a salary equal to or even below what you earned with your last employer, because this is what most companies do. Since you are unemployed, you will not be in a good position to argue.

Instead of purposefully placing yourself in a weak negotiating position, remember this:

IF YOU ARE PRESENTLY EMPLOYED, PROSPECTIVE EMPLOYERS WILL KNOW THEY MUST

MAKE IT WORTH YOUR WHILE TO CHANGE
COMPANIES.

Most offer an increase of at least ten percent of your present salary, though salary increases of twenty or thirty percent
are not uncommon. See the difference?

If you are still employed, decide what you want to do,
where you wish to work, and then wait until you have a solid
offer before turning in your resignation. Do not permit im-
patience or a hot temper to cost you several thousand dollars
in income as well as your finest negotiating point by quitting
your job before you have another. Keep prospective employers in a position where they must make an attractive offer
to you in order to convince you to work for them. This is
"career sense," and you would be doing a real favor to any
friend or relative who tells you she is thinking of quitting
her job by passing such information on to her. This is why
people should not wait until they are unemployed before
purchasing and reading this kind of book.

If you are unemployed, you can be the exception to the
rule only by making such a strong impression upon the hiring
authority that she disregards common practice because she
thinks you are a prize well worth paying extra for. Understand, however, the odds are stacked against your receiving
a higher salary offer than your last earnings, but it can hap-
pen if you follow, explicitly, the instructions given in the later
chapters on interview techniques and salary negotiations.

Charting A Course

Now that you have picked up a little job market savvy and
career sense, it is time to begin implementing your *TELE-
SEARCH* Plan. I'll give you a brief outline here so that you
will better understand our course, and then we'll move on to
the first step.

Your *TELESEARCH* Plan

1. Take the *TELESEARCH* Career Insight Quiz to determine the type of career positions that are most appealing to you, as well as the kind of companies or businesses you would most enjoy working for.

2. Define your market as broadly as possible.

3. Assemble and organize your lead sources.

4. Prepare your *TELESEARCH* List.

5. Plan and practice your *TELESEARCH* presentation and rebuttals.

6. *TELESEARCH* for interview appointments.

7. Prepare for each interview.

8. Interview for offers.

9. Follow up each interview.

10. After closing the best offer, notify other employers who may still be considering you for a position of your decision.

Now, start working at your new job, and store this book where you can easily locate it the next time you contemplate a job search.

TELESEARCH Career Insight Quiz

Get out a legal pad or several sheets of letter-size paper and answer the following questions as completely and candidly as you can. This quiz is for your own personal use, so allow plenty of time, be honest with yourself, and you will be better organized and better able to conduct your *TELESEARCH* with more confidence and far greater chance of success. Ask yourself the following questions:

1. WHY AM I UNEMPLOYED NOW OR READY TO CHANGE EMPLOYERS? Explain it to yourself, and it will be easier to explain it to a prospective employer.

2. WHAT DID I MOST ENJOY IN MY LAST (PRESENT) POSITION?

3. WHAT WERE MY GREATEST ACCOMPLISH-MENTS WITH THAT EMPLOYER?

4. WHAT DID I DISLIKE MOST IN MY LAST (PRES-ENT) JOB?

5. WHAT DO I REALLY WANT TO DO FOR A LIVING AND WHY?

6. WHAT IS MY LONG-RANGE PROFESSIONAL OB-JECTIVE?

7. WHAT CAREER POSITION WOULD BE THE NEXT LOGICAL STEP TOWARDS REACHING MY OBJEC-TIVE?

8. DO I NEED ADDITIONAL EDUCATION OR PROFESSIONAL TRAINING?

9. WHAT AM I BEST QUALIFIED TO DO NOW?

10. WHAT KIND OF COMPANIES OR BUSINESSES OF-FER THE BEST OPPORTUNITIES FOR SOMEONE WITH BOTH MY GOALS AND PROFESSIONAL EX-PERIENCE?

11. HOW MUCH SHOULD I REASONABLY EXPECT THEM TO PAY ME?

12. TO WHOM SHOULD I BE WORTH THE MOST?

13. WHERE WOULD I GO FOR THE "RIGHT OPPORTUNITY"?

14. I WANT TO WORK FOR A LARGE COMPANY BECAUSE....

15. I WANT TO WORK FOR A SMALL COMPANY BECAUSE....

16. REGARDLESS OF THE SIZE OF THE COMPANY, MY NEW EMPLOYER SHOULD BE ABLE TO OFFER....

17. IN EXCHANGE FOR WHICH, I CAN OFFER MY NEW EMPLOYER....

18. IF I COULD FIND THE "IDEAL JOB" FOR MYSELF, WHAT IS THE MINIMUM SALARY THAT I WOULD ACCEPT TO START?

19. THE TYPE OF CAREER POSITION THAT I WOULD ACCEPT IMMEDIATELY WITHOUT ANY HESITATION, IF OFFERED, IS: (A)

    MY SECOND CHOICE WOULD BE: (B)

    MY THIRD CHOICE WOULD BE: (C)

20. OTHER CAREER POSITIONS THAT I WOULD ENJOY ALMOST AS MUCH ARE....

Obviously, these are very personal questions that may require a great deal of soul-searching on your part, but I am sure you will understand the pattern and purpose of them. If you simply relax and write down honest answers, you may be surprised at your own capability for solving seemingly unsolvable personal problems, and organizing your conscious and subconscious desires, dreams, and thoughts into meaningful goals and objectives. No, I am not entering the metaphysical. If you approach this simple quiz seriously, without time limits or distractions, you will experience the "magic" that people often feel when writing down their innermost thoughts.

If you are among those fortunate enough to know exactly what you want, it will not take you very long to complete the quiz. If, on the other hand, you have been confused about your career goals or lacked direction and purpose, then you should not be alarmed if it takes you several hours or even days to complete this quiz to your satisfaction. Hours or days spent here can save you years of frustration, so once again, I urge you to take your time.

Some of you may find that the career you desire most seems unattainable. Let me pass on a positive thought that I picked up from Napoleon Hill's book *Think And Grow Rich*, and, I might add, that the history of mankind has verified millions of times. Simply explained, it goes like this:

YOUR MIND WOULD NOT FORMULATE A STRONG DESIRE FOR SOMETHING THAT IT IS INCAPABLE OF ACHIEVING. ALL OF THE RE-SOURCES NECESSARY FOR THE ATTAINMENT OF YOUR GOAL ARE WITHIN YOUR GRASP, AND WILL REVEAL THEMSELVES TO YOU IF YOU WILL SET YOUR SIGHTS UPON THAT GOAL AND STRIVE PERSISTENTLY TOWARDS ITS ACHIEVE-MENT.

In other words, you can have what you really want if you are willing to work for it and do not quit until you get it. My own life has borne this out, and I do not know how anyone could look back through history at the countless astonishing human achievements and dismiss the truth of these words. Compared to space travel, computers, nuclear power, genetics, and even the pyramids—finding a meaningful career for yourself is a small task, indeed, and one that is easily within your grasp.

3
Fundamentals Of TELESEARCH

After completing your Career Insight Quiz, you should have selected three types of career positions that would be most satisfactory for you. We will call these three choices positions "A," "B," and "C," respectively; with "A" representing your first choice, "B" your second, and "C" your third. If you also named some additional types of career positions as being equally enjoyable, then label them accordingly. These will provide easy reference points as we proceed with your *TELESEARCH* Plan.

Define And Expand Your Market

Now that you know what you want to do, you will need to determine which companies will be hiring for each type of position you have chosen so that you can prepare your *TELE-*

SEARCH List of companies to contact. Research and planning are fundamental to the success of your job search and, though time-consuming, will actually save you a lot of time in the long run.

Beginning with position "A," write down all of the types of businesses and companies you can think of that employ people in that occupation. Unless you are changing career fields completely, competitors of your last or present employer will probably head your list. What kind of business are they in? Who are their customers? Whom do they buy their supplies and raw materials from? What kinds of service companies do they do business with? How about similar industries? If your employer manufactured automobiles, for instance, what other types of heavy equipment manufacturers in your area might employ similar manufacturing methods and, therefore, might hire people with a background similar to yours?

Look over the Help Wanted ads in the Sunday classifieds of your local newspapers. What kinds of companies advertise for people to work in your chosen field? Back issues can be just as helpful because, at this point, we are not so interested in investigating current openings as in determining which types of companies usually employ people in your field. We will get to those specific openings later.

The Yellow Pages may also prove helpful in defining your market because they list businesses according to the product they sell or service they perform. Occupational guides and directories, which also discuss the various kinds of businesses that employ people in a particular occupation, may be found in your local library. Former co-workers, friends, and relatives may also provide helpful suggestions for expanding your market.

Once you have come up with a sizable list for position "A," compile similar lists for "B" and "C." At this point, remember, we are not so concerned with the *names* of particular companies as we are with the *types* of prospective employers. After you have targeted your market, we will assemble your lead sources to determine which specific companies you should contact, as well as the names of particular hiring authorities you should talk with.

Lead Sources

Basically, there are two kinds of lead sources that you will use. The first will provide information about specific openings. The second will provide names and phone numbers of particular companies and their respective hiring authorities. Often you will use the two together, because even if you learn of a particular opening at a company, your source may not know the name of the foreman, supervisor, manager, department head, or executive to whom you would report if you got the job.

Help Wanted ads are one of the best examples of why you may need to use both sources. These ads will often include the name of a secretary, corporate recruiter, or personnel representative as the person to contact rather than the actual decision maker. If you are going to outmaneuver the competition for an opening, then you should avoid contacting a firm's personnel department, unless there is absolutely no other way to go. Remember:

PERSONNEL SCREENS BUT MANAGEMENT HIRES!

Generally, it is the personnel interviewer's responsibility to determine whether there is any reason why an applicant should *not* be hired. It is the manager or department head who actually decides which job candidate will work for him, and it is this person who will be most concerned with finding the best employee because he will be credited by his boss for operating the department at maximum efficiency. He is the real hiring authority, and if he wants you for his department, he will make sure you are properly taken care of by his firm's personnel department.

Finding Openings

Help Wanted ads are one of the finest sources for locating current openings. I know I stated earlier that answering classified ads provided one of the worst chances of success for most people, but that is because most people simply call without discovering the real hiring authority. If, however, you research the company and contact the actual hiring authority rather than the company's personnel department, these ads can be a very useful source.

Of course, most of the Help Wanted ads will appear in the classified section of your local Sunday newspapers, but many papers also run ads in their business section. Advertisements for male employment opportunities may also appear in the sports pages and ads for female employment may also be found in the women's section. Trade magazines that cater to your particular industry often have Help Wanted advertisements in the back of each issue. The Tuesday edition of *The Wall Street Journal* has a substantial Help Wanted section, entitled "The MART," listing executive and professional openings. A new publication, *The National Business Employment Weekly*, compiles all of the openings advertised in all editions of *The Wall Street Journal* each week, and should be available at your local newsstand each Sunday. This publication, to which I have been a contributor, often includes helpful articles on job hunting.

Federal, state, and local community employment offices will know of openings, as will high school career counseling offices. Your college or university alumni society may have a placement office, and there are private trade associations for virtually every kind of profession that list openings. In addition, there are non-profit organizations that specialize in finding jobs for various groups of people. Forty-Plus, for example, assists in locating employment for people over forty.

Friends, relatives, former co-workers, and former supervisors will often learn of openings from their own contacts within their respective career fields. Think about the different contacts you might have in your church and the various civic organizations in your community. Bankers, who often learn of expansion plans by their business customers, could prove very helpful to you in your search for openings. You will probably come up with even more ideas for sources as you read this; write your ideas down as they occur to you.

Pay particular attention to the business section of your local newspaper or local business publication for news of expansion plans of local businesses in your chosen field. Companies that are expanding will definitely need to hire more people.

Contact Information

Once you learn of an opening, try to find out the name of the boss for that particular department within the company. I mentioned earlier that your source may not always know whom to contact, but often they will. If available from your source, write down the name of the company, the hiring authority, and the phone number where he can be reached.

If you cannot learn this information from your prime source, your local library or Chamber of Commerce has directories of companies in that business from which you can learn the name of the person you need to contact. Trade directories are published for virtually every industry and can be found in any public library.

Inform your librarian that you need trade directories that list the key personnel in each corporation. I would like to give you a list of all directories but there are thousands. Your local Chamber of Commerce and various professional organizations will usually publish very informative business directories. Dun & Bradstreet and Standard & Poor's both publish exhaustive national directories of major corporations in the United States, but each industry has its own, more detailed directory showing a breakdown of the departments within every company listed. Most will list the names of all officers and major department heads along with the address and phone number of each branch office. Directories of various manufacturers will normally give the names of plant

37

managers and the key management staff of each plant. Most directories have their own coding system, so read the instructions carefully.

Your TELESEARCH List

Now you are ready to prepare your *TELESEARCH* List. Set up a few pages in a notebook or legal pad. (*See Exhibit A.*) If you have access to a copier, run off about a dozen or so copies.

Actually, I would suggest you make up three separate lists; one each for positions A, B, and C. First, note the companies with known openings. Then look up the phone numbers, names, and titles of the hiring authorities and write them down (under "Contact"). Add to your list all the other companies included in the same sections of the directories as those with known openings. They, too, might be able to use someone with your background and should be contacted.

In fact, list every company you can find that might employ people in the type of career position (or positions) you are seeking. Recheck the Yellow Pages for any other companies you should contact, and look up the necessary contact information in the trade directories. Earlier, you researched the types of businesses that employed people in your occupation. Now, add to your *TELESEARCH* List all of the companies in each of those fields.

If you cannot find the name of the supervisor, manager, or department head you need to contact, list the name of the executive in charge of the particular branch, or department. You may then call this executive and ask him for the name of the department head you are seeking. When you do reach the proper contact, you can truthfully say that you were referred to him by one of the "top brass," who may very well be your contact's boss.

Compiling your *TELESEARCH* List is important because you will not have to stop between each call to look up contact information and phone numbers. As you go through your calls, you will develop a kind of rhythm that aids your delivery and maintains your enthusiasm. Your expertise will improve

Exhibit A

TELESEARCH LIST

COMPANIES TO CALL

DATE_____   Type of position_____

Phone	Company	Contact	Title	Source	Results

with each call. Preparing your *TELESEARCH* List in advance helps you keep up a fast pace, and you will notice a marked improvement in your results. Using this method, a professional recruiter can contact twenty or thirty employers in one morning, and there is no reason why you cannot take full advantage of the same system.

Employers In Other Cities

Unless you are absolutely opposed to relocating for a better opportunity, you will also want to include out-of-town companies in your *TELESEARCH* List. Many of the trade directories you have been using give the names of companies in similar businesses that are located in other cities. The national directories published by Dun & Bradstreet or Standard & Poor's list the larger corporations. Your local telephone company's central office should have Yellow Pages for all major cities and you can use them at the company's office. Of course, Yellow Pages will not provide the name of a hiring authority, but you can get it with a phone call.

You should not be too concerned with long-distance telephone rates. Place all long-distance calls person to person to the hiring authority. Although that person will most likely be busy the first time you call, you can leave your name and number—free of charge. The operator will hassle with the secretary, and since most companies consider it a professional courtesy to pay for return calls, the majority of your conversations will not cost you anything. For this reason, person-to-person calls are even cheaper than direct-dial or discount long-distance systems.

One of the greatest advantages of person-to-person calls is that you ask for someone by title only—Eastern Sales Manager, Vice President of Finance, Plant Manager, Office Manager, etc.—if you do not know the hiring authority's name. The operator will go through channels to locate the hiring authority without charging you anything for the call until you actually begin speaking to the individual you are trying to reach. Person to person can be a really good deal.

Many out-of-town employers want to see a resume. I will show you ways of avoiding this with local employers, but an employer in another city will probably want to review your resume before agreeing to pay your travel expenses for an interview. Your chances of success will be greatly improved if you call first, however, and establish contact rather than simply mailing your resume to employers indiscriminately.

When making long-distance calls, pay attention to time zones. The telephone directory usually includes a map of time zones for quick reference. If you live on the East Coast, you may want to schedule your West Coast calls last (8:30 A.M. in New York is normally 5:30 A.M. in Los Angeles). The same advice would apply in reverse for late afternoon calls from the West Coast to the East Coast. Take the time to plan your calls in advance, and time zones will not be a problem.

Outmaneuvering The Competition

As you complete your *TELESEARCH* List, do not be too concerned about whether or not the companies you have listed have advertised openings. First, you should plan to contact every company in a particular field whether or not they have advertised an opening. If they have advertised an opening, so much the better. If they have not, it does not mean that they are not looking to hire someone. Many companies begin recruiting by listing their job openings internally to see if any of their employees would have any interest in and be qualified for the position, or might at least be able to recommend someone for the job. Some companies will list the opening with their favorite search firms or agencies instead of advertising publicly. In any event, it may take several weeks between the time a supervisor notifies the personnel department of an opening and the time an ad actually appears in the classifieds.

41

One major advantage of contacting all companies in a particular industry is that you will probably learn of openings before they work their way through channels to become public knowledge.

To arrange an interview, always call the supervisor you think you would probably report to within a company. If he does not have an opening in his department, be sure to ask if he knows of any openings in other departments. Does he know the name of the supervisor to contact? Does he know of any openings with any of his firm's competitors? Pick his brain for all the information you can gather. If you get no positive results from the hiring authorities you have contacted within a particular company, call the company's personnel department to learn if there are any company-wide openings for someone with your experience. In this manner, you will be able to take maximum advantage of each company on your list. Just remember to go through personnel last—after exhausting all other possibilities. I realize I'll not be too popular with personnel people after this book is published but, as Sherman said, "War is Hell," and when the national unemployment figure hovers around ten percent and you are among those who are unemployed, job hunting is war!

If someone from a company's personnel department should catch you going around him, apologize courteously, with deep sincerity, and explain that you would be more than happy to meet with him the following morning in his office—unless the afternoon would be more convenient for him. This way you can still set up an interview appointment, and the employer will most likely admire your aggressiveness and resourcefulness. Just tell the personnel representative that your source did not advise you to contact the company's personnel department, which is true—I didn't.

Getting Ready

For *TELESEARCH*, you will need a quiet place from which to make your phone calls. A desk would be helpful because you will need to make notes as you go along. Make sure that your TV and stereo are turned off and ask your family to hold down the noise. Background noises can be distracting to you as well as to the person on the other end of the line. I love my daughter, Tesia, but nothing can destroy my professionalism faster than the sound of a three-year-old crying or yelling in the background during a business call.

Plan your day so that you can make your calls in the morning and answer calls in the afternoon. If you know you will be out, make sure someone will be near the phone to take your calls, and instruct them to *write down the caller's name, company, and phone number*. If you make your calls in the morning and leave your name and number but your call is not returned by 2:00 P.M., call again that afternoon.

Have a calendar in front of you when placing your calls. Select convenient times for interviews each day for one to two weeks in advance. This way you can arrange appointments quickly and smoothly without long delays or frantic interruptions during your conversations. Try not to schedule more than three interviews for any one day and allow plenty of time to research the company and position before an interview.

Keep your *TELESEARCH* List in front of you at all times and promptly record the results of each call. One other advantage of writing down each call is that when one of your calls is returned, you can quickly check your *TELESEARCH* List to see why you called that particular person and to check the name of the company. This can become a problem when making twenty or thirty calls in one day, but you can easily handle it if you keep a clear, legible record of each call.

Monday, Tuesday, or Wednesday mornings are the best times to make your calls. The earlier in the week the better, giving both you and your contact more time to plan the week before schedules are full. Start at 8 or 8:30 in the morning or as early as people in your profession start their day. I also prefer Friday mornings because you can usually catch the hiring authority in a good mood while he is thinking about the weekend, and it is easy to arrange an appointment for early the following week.

Write down your basic presentation and standard rebuttals (they will be discussed in the next chapter), and keep them in front of you when placing your calls. Practice your presentation and rebuttals until you are satisfied with your style of delivery. A tape recorder is a valuable training aid for practicing your *TELESEARCH* techniques. You may wish to purchase a telephone pick-up (microphone) from an electronics store so that you can record your conversations. You can then replay these recorded conversations to evaluate and improve your technique. In addition, you won't miss any important facts or directions for finding the hiring authority's office.

Company Contact Record

As you begin arranging interviews, you will want to record important facts about each company you contact for quick reference. Exhibit B is a Company Contact Record that is very similar to the Job Order form which most recruiters and personnel consultants use to keep records of their clients and their applicants' progress in interviews. You may wish to run off a few copies of this form or set up index cards to record vital facts.

Although most of the spaces are self-explanatory, I would like to call your attention to three sections that have a special purpose beyond the obvious. "Company's products," "Customers," and "Competitors" are included not only to help you understand the prospective employer's business but also to increase your list of prospects.

Other companies who work with the same products, competitors of the firm you are interviewing with and the customers of these companies might also be interested in hiring someone with your background and expertise. Be sure to record the names of these firms for future reference and then add them to your *TELESEARCH* List after researching the contact information in trade directories.

Exhibit B

COMPANY CONTACT RECORD

*Company*_____*Phone*_____
*Address*_____
*Directions for locating*_____

*Date of interview*_____*Time*_____*Arranged by*_____
_____*Name of interviewer*_____
*Title*_____*Names and titles of other contacts:*
_____
_____

*Title of position*_____
*Job description*_____
_____

*Company's products*_____
*Customers*_____
*Competitors*_____
*Years in business*_____*Employees in co.*_____*Department*_____
*Home office location*_____
*Resume sent?*_____*Date*_____*Follow-up call?*_____*Date*_____
*Results*_____
*Mailgram sent?*_____*Date*_____*Second interview date*_____
*Results*_____
*Third interview date*_____*Results*_____
_____*Fourth interview date*____
*Results*_____

45

The rest of this form will help you keep up with your progress as you go through the interview process. The more companies you interview with, the more you will need to maintain good records in order to follow up properly with each firm. Keep these forms handy as you begin making your calls and you will start your *TELESEARCH* more professionally and be better organized from the beginning. (See Exhibit B.)

Overcoming "Phone Phobia"

Some job seekers are so afraid of using the telephone that they will not even make calls. Generally, the reason they are so afraid is because they have not made the calls. They have never taken that first step for fear of failure. They allow these fears to defeat them.

No one can ever expect to find success or even much happiness if they go through life afraid to try something because they might fail. The only way people ever become good at anything is by trying and trying again until they learn to do it right. *TELESEARCH* is no different.

You will fail—occasionally. You will make mistakes—in the beginning. You will probably embarrass yourself—once or twice. You will forget someone's name, call them by the wrong name, forget the name of the company or what business they are in. You may even get someone on the line (as I have) and draw a complete blank, forgetting whom you called or why you called. You may even call the same employer twice, as I have done. Later, you will laugh about these very same human mistakes. Most likely, the hiring authorities will laugh right along with you and even try harder to assist you because we all respect and naturally want to help those who are really trying to help themselves. Remember, those hiring authorities are just as human as you are and none of them is perfect, either.

Do not waste your valuable time worrying about failing or

making mistakes. Accept the fact that you will make a few blunders along the way, but also accept the fact that you will get better as you go along. Each time you talk with an employer it will get easier, until you realize just how much fun you can have talking with other professionals in the career field of your choice. *TELESEARCH* is easy—if you let it be. It will provide you with a rare opportunity to get to know the people who count in your business and actually establish lasting friendships with many of them. Just make up your mind to enjoy these conversations and have a good time. Relax and be yourself; be friendly and people will return your friendship.

You may not realize it, but you will actually have a tremendous advantage over the people on the other end of the line in your *TELESEARCH* conversations. You know what you called for in the first place—they don't. You know exactly what you will say and where the conversation will be headed—they don't. You even know what *they* will probably say and you already have an answer for it. This knowledge and the techniques and rebuttals you will learn in the next chapter will give you a powerful edge. You will actually learn to control your *TELESEARCH* conversations to get the results you want. Once learned, these lessons will help you in your dealings with people for the rest of your life.

If you have only half as much faith in me as I have in you, you will be successful. I mean that. I've taught these techniques to all kinds of people in all kinds of occupations; learned from their mistakes and questions; and then applied those lessons to thousands of conversations. I have discussed these techniques with professionals in my field and we have pooled our experience to come up with solutions to problems that work effectively in virtually any conceivable situation. These have been checked and double-checked until the margin for error has been reduced to less than ten percent!

Believe me, I would not have sweated over these pages for almost two years—nor would I ask you to plow through them—if I did not truly believe that you could learn these

47

techniques and apply them successfully. So, let's forget about "phone phobia" or failing, and instead, concentrate upon succeeding.

4
TELESEARCH In Action

The best way to avoid mistakes, overcome fears or nervousness, and reap the maximum benefit from your *TELESEARCH* is by forming good *TELESEARCH* habits in the beginning. In other words, follow the procedures and practice the skills and techniques outlined in this book persistently until they become habitual. Once these habits are firmly established, you will follow them automatically as you concentrate your efforts and focus your attention upon the purpose of your *TELESEARCH*—obtaining meaningful interview appointments.

Budget Your Time

Managing your time effectively will greatly increase your odds of success. As I said earlier, you should always prepare your

TELESEARCH List in advance and plan to make your calls in the mornings. Have enough self-discipline to avoid letting anything else prevent you from completing your calls as planned. Try not to plan anything else for those mornings you intend to contact employers by phone. Use afternoons for research, errands, chores, etc.

Inform the other members of your household that you wish to make all of your calls without interruption. Until you feel comfortable and confident in your delivery, I would suggest that each day you plan your first three to five calls for those "C" (third-choice) positions from your Career Insight Quiz. After you have practiced your presentation and rebuttals with these employers and gotten over those "butterflies," then start calling the "A" prospects. Go through your list quickly by contacting ten or fifteen employers in a stretch. It is much easier to stay "up" if you immediately follow each call with another, rather than pausing for breaks between calls. It is too easy to become discouraged during breaks as you sit and stare at the telephone. Fears and nervousness begin to creep up on you and destroy your confidence. Establish a fast pace, and your presentation will be more enthusiastic and positive.

Plan Your Presentation

Think about what you are going to say in advance and write it down. Keep it simple. Remember:

ALL YOU WANT TO GAIN FROM THE CALL IS AN INTERVIEW APPOINTMENT. DO NOT TRY TO INTERVIEW, SCREEN THE COMPANY, READ YOUR RESUME, ETC., OVER THE TELEPHONE.

Just set up an interview appointment and get off the line. This is the best way I know of impressing your prospective employers with your respect for both their time and yours.

Whenever possible, try to get on a first-name basis from the start. It seems to relax the conversation and quickly helps establish real communication. If you have not been able to learn the hiring authority's first name from any of your sources, ask the secretary or receptionist who answers the phone. If you use formal titles, i.e., Mr., Mrs. or Ms., you may waste valuable time by becoming entangled in lengthy introductions or explanations. As a "born and bred Southerner" I respect professional courtesies and etiquette, but a little familiarity here can overcome a multitude of objections and distractions. The rare individual who might be offended by your use of his or her given name is probably too "stuffy" to be the kind of boss you want to work for anyway.

Remember to get to the point immediately when you have the hiring authority on the line. She will probably be involved in something else when she picks up the phone, so you must get her attention in the first ten to fifteen seconds or her thoughts will return to whatever she was doing when you called. Below are three examples of brief, simple, but effective presentations:

> Sue, my name is ———— ————. I have ——— years experience in our business and I'd like to stop by your office to discuss working for you. Would tomorrow morning around eleven be a good time for your schedule or would after lunch be better?

> Jim, my name is———— ————. I've got——— years experience with one of your firm's competitors and I'm thinking of making a change. I'd like to arrange an appointment for a meeting in your office to discuss working for you. Would eleven o'clock tomorrow morning be convenient or would tomorrow afternoon be better for your schedule?

> Larry, my name is ———— ————. I'd like to stop by your office tomorrow afternoon to talk about

working for you as a ———. Would two o'clock be convenient or would after four be better for you?

Note:

> YOU DID NOT MENTION AN ADVERTISED OPEN-
> ING OR EVEN ASK IF THERE WAS AN OPENING,
> IF THE COMPANY WAS HIRING, OR ANY OTHER
> SCREEN-OUT-TYPE QUESTIONS.

The employer will tell you if any of these things are important or might pose an obstacle to arranging an interview. You simply asked the most convenient time for a meeting, offering a choice of two time slots (convenient to your schedule). This is the only decision you want the employer to make at present. The old sales trick of offering a "choice of two" is called a "forced response" question and is most effective when setting interview appointments. If the times you suggested are not acceptable, then offer another choice of two:

> Well, if not tomorrow, how about Thursday morn-
> ing or Friday afternoon? Which looks best on your
> calendar? At two o'clock or four?

Remember, you are not calling to find out if there is an opening or what the company's hiring plans are. You want an appointment. If she positively cannot hire anyone, she will tell you. If, on the other hand, the hiring authority is impressed with your style and agrees to an interview, she may think you could be just the person to replace an employee she has been dissatisfied with. If you start off by asking about hiring plans or openings, the hiring authority might simply refer you to the personnel department. Instead, by calling her and asking to meet with her personally, you will impress her with your resourcefulness and she will probably be curious enough to agree to the meeting so she can see you herself. If you simply "called about the ad in the paper"— like everyone else—you will be referred to personnel or the employee who has been assigned to screen calls. I am not saying that you will not be screened, but this way you have a better chance of starting out with the real decision maker.

KEEP YOUR PRESENTATION SIMPLE AND CON-CENTRATE UPON WHAT YOU ARE AFTER—AN APPOINTMENT FOR AN INTERVIEW.

Smile

Telephone marketing experts and professional recruiters have learned that they can make their voices sound more pleasant and much friendlier if they smile when speaking over the phone. Think about the person you are speaking with and talk *to* that person, not *at* them. Sometimes it helps to try to picture the other person in your mind. Be sure to relax and make it a friendly conversation. Smiling makes it easier.

Be Enthusiastic

You cannot expect the hiring authority to get excited about meeting you if you do not sound enthusiastic about yourself. Your enthusiasm can overcome a multitude of objections and help get the employer so interested in meeting you that she will agree to an interview appointment without hesitation. If you have any doubts about your ability to sound enthusiastic on every call, there is another old sales trick that may be helpful to you.

Sales professionals who present the same product every day must be able to turn on the enthusiasm in each presentation, regardless of how they feel or how many times they have to say the same things. You can learn to do what they do:

SLIGHTLY RAISE THE VOLUME AND SPEED OF YOUR VOICE TO SOUND ENTHUSIASTIC.

Be sure not to shout or talk so fast that you cannot be understood. Enthusiasm is a very powerful tool and highly contagious when used effectively. Practice with your spouse, a friend, or a tape recorder until your presentation sounds enthusiastic and genuine, not "canned." If you memorize your presentation, and I suggest that you do, it will not sound canned as long as you vary the pitch of your voice while you speak.

A friendly, enthusiastic voice will make you sound more confident and thereby strengthen the employer's desire to meet you. Be yourself. Be careful not to sound like a used car salesman on a late-night TV commercial. Just be the friendliest, most confident, enthusiastic "self" you can be, and if there is even the remotest possibility the employer needs someone in her department, you will get your appointment.

Maintain Control

You must maintain control of the conversation if you are to achieve the desired results. In order to do this effectively, you will need to respond to the most commonly asked questions and objections smoothly (plan in advance), then quickly bring the conversation back to setting an interview appointment. The easiest way of keeping the conversation on the desired track is by implementing what I call Truitt's Law, for want of a better name.

Truitt's Law

THE MOST IMPORTANT THINGS TO REMEMBER WHEN YOU ENCOUNTER QUESTIONS OR OB-JECTIONS ARE TO STAY FRIENDLY, BE COOP-ERATIVE, AND *ANSWER A QUESTION WITH A QUESTION TO REGAIN CONTROL OF A CONVER-SATION.*

54

Yes, you can actually control the conversation and where it is heading—if you apply yourself. As I said in Chapter Three, you have the advantage over the person on the other end of the line because you know what the call is about, what will be said, and which questions will probably be asked. You can anticipate most of the questions you will hear and plan your responses ahead of time. Then when you roll off your answers and finish them with questions of your own, the other person will have to pause to consider a reply, giving you time to prepare your next question. At this point you are in complete control of the conversation.

As an example, let us imagine that you have called an employer and she asks how you happened to get her name. You may wish to structure your answer along these lines:

> Let's just say that I've heard you were a fine employer and would like to meet with you, personally, to discuss working in your department. Would tomorrow morning be convenient or would after lunch be better for you?

Questions and objections may come from a receptionist, secretary, or employer. Below are some of the more common questions you are likely to hear and some effective answers, along with more examples of how you can regain control of phone conversations with some questions of your own.

Questions & Objections from a Secretary or Receptionist

1. QUESTION: WHAT'S IT ABOUT? WHO ARE YOU WITH? DOES SHE KNOW YOU?

YOUR RESPONSE: "Just tell her that ——— ——— is holding on the line. Is she in?"

2. OBJECTION: SHE IS OUT; TIED UP; IN A MEETING; ON THE OTHER LINE.

YOUR RESPONSE: "Tell her —— —— called. Do you know when she'll be free to return my call?"

3. OBJECTION: SHE IS NO LONGER WITH US; NO LONGER IN THIS DEPARTMENT.

YOUR RESPONSE: "Who's got that job, now? Do you know her first name? What do her friends call her? May I speak with her, please?"

Objections From The Hiring Authority

1. OBJECTION: I'M BUSY.

YOUR RESPONSE: "I know it's a busy time. Could we meet after hours then...say, tomorrow or would late Friday afternoon be better for you?"
(or)
"I beg your pardon; may I call back this afternoon or would tomorrow morning be better for you?"

2. OBJECTION: WE'RE NOT HIRING NOW.

YOUR RESPONSE: "Yes, I'd heard you had a fine organization. In fact, that's exactly why I thought you could give me some good advice as to my best career move. Could we

get together tomorrow afternoon after work or would the
weekend be better for you?"*

3. OBJECTION: CALL OUR PERSONNEL DE-
PARTMENT.

YOUR RESPONSE: "I'm going to see them tomorrow
afternoon. I was hoping that since
we're both in —— and speak
the same language, we might get
together to see if I could help
your organization, and you could
then direct me to the right people in personnel. May I stop by
your office for a few minutes be-
forehand...say, around eleven
or would right after lunch be better for your schedule?"

4. OBJECTION: WE'VE ALREADY TALKED
TO A LOT OF PEOPLE AND
WE'RE GOING TO MAKE OUR
SELECTION FROM THOSE.

YOUR RESPONSE: "I understand your reasoning,
but I can do that job well, and
with business as tight as it is, you
want to find the best employee
for your money. I'll run by there
tomorrow morning if you like, or
would right after lunch be better
for you?"

---

* The employer may know of openings in another department within
his company or at one of his firm's competitors. The employer could be
so impressed with you and your experience that he may decide to replace
a "weak link" in his department with you. It is worth a shot, anyway. If
he is greatly impressed by you, he may give you a personal recommendation
to one of his friends or associates who may very well be able to hire you.

5. OBJECTION: WE JUST LAID OFF TEN PEO-
                   PLE FROM MY DEPART-
                   MENT.

YOUR RESPONSE: "I'd heard you were streamlining
                   your operation. In fact, I wanted
                   to meet with you tomorrow
                   morning to discuss ways I might
                   help make your department even
                   more efficient. Could we meet at
                   nine or would just before lunch
                   be more convenient for you?"*

6. OBJECTION   BUSINESS IS TOO SLOW
                   RIGHT NOW.

YOUR RESPONSE: "Yes, and now is the time you
                   want your department running
                   at maximum efficiency in order
                   to save on expenses. I'd like to
                   meet with you in your office to-
                   morrow afternoon to discuss this,
                   unless Friday morning would be
                   better for you. Which would be
                   the most convenient time for your
                   schedule?"*

7. OBJECTION: WE'VE GOT A HIRING
                   FREEZE ON RIGHT NOW.

YOUR RESPONSE: "Yes, a lot of companies have
                   done that but the smart employ-
                   ers are taking advantage of this

---

* The employer may know of openings in another department within
his company or at one of his firm's competitors. The employer could be
so impressed with you and your experience that he may decide to replace
a "weak link" in his department with you. It is worth a shot, anyway. If
he is greatly impressed by you, he may give you a personal recommendation
to one of his friends or associates who may very well be able to hire you.

58

situation to upgrade the quality of their departments. Could we get together and discuss this face to face tomorrow afternoon, or would Wednesday morning be better for your schedule?"*

8. OBJECTION: I HAVE TOO MUCH WORK TO DO.

YOUR RESPONSE: I'd sure like to help you with that work load. Could we get together tomorrow around four or would Thursday morning be a better time?"

9. OBJECTION: SEND ME YOUR RESUME.

YOUR RESPONSE: "Actually, I just learned of this opportunity and haven't had time to put one together. May I fill out your company's application before we meet tomorrow afternoon, or would Wednesday morning be better for your schedule?"

(or)

"I've been working with one of your firm's competitors and I'd prefer to keep this as confidential as possible. Could I bring it with me when we meet? Would

---

* The employer may know of openings in another department within his company or at one of his firm's competitors. The employer could be so impressed with you and your experience that he may decide to replace a "weak link" in his department with you. It is worth a shot, anyway. If he is greatly impressed by you, he may give you a personal recommendation to one of his friends or associates who may very well be able to hire you.

two o'clock Thursday be a good time or would four-thirty be better?"

(or)

"Sue, there are so many resumes coming into your company these days, I think we might both save a lot of time if we got together, face to face in your office tomorrow morning, or would late Thursday afternoon be better for you?"

10. OBJECTION: FRANKLY, YOU WOULD JUST BE WASTING YOUR TIME.

YOUR RESPONSE: "You may be right but you sound like the kind of manager who likes to have the best employees she can find. I know your company and I'm willing to take my chances in an interview. Could we try it tomorrow morning around ten or would three in the afternoon be better for you?"*

Of course, none of these rebuttals will work every time. Would you settle for seventy-five percent? Fifty percent? One out of five? They will help you get what you called for in the first place—an interview appointment.

---

* The employer may know of openings in another department within his company or at one of his firm's competitors. The employer could be so impressed with you and your experience that he may decide to replace a "weak link" in his department with you. It is worth a shot, anyway. If he is greatly impressed by you, he may give you a personal recommendation to one of his friends or associates who may very well be able to hire you.

Positive Questions

All questions do not carry negative connotations. If the hiring authority starts firing questions at you about your background, education, or experience—you know she is interested and has something in mind. Here again, turn those questions into an interview appointment and get off the phone as quickly as you can. Do not try to interview over the telephone or oversell yourself. You could say something like the following in a low, almost secretive voice:

> Yes, I've had ———— years of experience but listen, I'm using a private line right now. Could we meet in your office tomorrow morning, where I can speak freely and answer your questions in greater detail or would early afternoon be more convenient for you?

You want to meet the employer face to face so that you can use your appearance, professionalism, positive attitude and qualifications to persuade her to make you an attractive offer.

Use the telephone to arrange interview appointments; use the interview to get offers.

Ask For Referrals

If you cannot arrange an interview, ask for referrals. You might say:

> Sue, I do appreciate your taking your valuable time to talk with me, and I am truly sorry I won't have a chance to work with you. Who do you know that might use a veteran in our business with ———— years experience? Do you have their phone number? Who's in charge over there? What do her friends call her? May I use your name as a referral?

Always try to gain *something* from every call you make. If the hiring authority you are talking to cannot tell you about a specific opening, ask if she knows which companies in her field are expanding. Ask about customers and suppliers as well and new businesses that are just starting up. Be friendly and courteous, and she may even want to take your name and number in case something turns up. Finish your call by requesting permission to call back in a week or so to learn if she has heard of any new opportunities. Pretty soon, you may have a small army scouting opportunities for you. This can only help your cause.

Control Your Attitude

You should never get into an argument with a prospective employer over the telephone. Agree with what she says and then make your point. Did you notice that almost all of the rebuttals shown earlier began with "Yes," "I understand," "I see what you mean" or "I agree"? Learn to begin each rebuttal by agreeing with the other person's point, and you will never start an argument. It takes two to argue. If you do get into a disagreement with a prospective employer over the phone, you will lose even if you are right. Sure, you might win the argument, but you will not get an interview or even any help with referrals.

Occasionally, you will encounter rudeness during your *TELESEARCH*. If you make enough calls, you will always find a jerk. Just laugh it off and mark it down for what it truly is—ignorance. Do not let some rude ignoramus make you blow your next ten calls by your reacting to her insults. That is what she wants. If you should run into this kind of situation or feel your temper getting out of control, politely get off the phone, take a breather, and relax. Some of these people will try to make you feel small, second class, or as if you are stealing their valuable time. All they are doing is displaying their inflated egos. Swapping insults with this kind of person will only lower you to her level. Be professional.

Laugh, hang up, and make your next call unperturbed. That is how you beat those people at their own game.

IF YOU RUN INTO REPEATED RUDENESS OR NEGATIVE RESPONSES, IT'S NOT THEM—IT'S YOU.

You may be too "uptight." Loosen up and smile. You will be amazed at how many nice people you can meet over the phone. Control your attitude and stay enthusiastic. Even the calls that do not produce interviews can end up giving you new ideas or worthwhile leads, if you keep a good attitude. You may set no more than five to ten interviews from thirty or forty calls, but five is a lot and ten is more than you will ever need if you follow the interview instructions in the upcoming chapters. This is where preparation, practice, and controlling your attitude really pay off.

Be Persistent

Most of today's true success stories are, in fact, tales of persistence. All of us admire those who overcome adversity and obstacles by sticking with something until they finally succeed.

TELESEARCH is no different. Set goals for yourself as you make your calls. Try to arrange three to five interviews per session. Set a minimum goal of at least two interviews per day and tell yourself that you will not quit until you get them. Go through your "A" list first. Next, call the names on your "B" list, and then finish with your "C" list. As you hear of opportunities from hiring authorities, add these to a new *TELESEARCH* List; find out the contact information you need and call the proper hiring authorities.

As I said at the beginning of this chapter, practice these skills and techniques until they become automatic—a habit. Write your presentation and rebuttals in your own words and memorize them. If you do, you will never be at a loss as to what to say or how to overcome a question or objection. This helps build your confidence, too. Here is a review of the most important *TELESEARCH* habits you need for success:

Successful *TELESEARCH* Habits

1. PLAN YOUR *TELESEARCH* LIST IN ADVANCE.
2. *TELESEARCH* IN THE MORNING.
3. SET GOALS OF AT LEAST TWO INTERVIEWS PER DAY.
4. KNOW WHAT YOU ARE GOING TO SAY.
5. GET TO THE POINT IMMEDIATELY.
6. SMILE AND BE FRIENDLY.
7. SPEAK WITH ENTHUSIASM.
8. OFFER A "CHOICE OF TWO."
9. KEEP CENTERED ON WHAT YOU WANT—AN INTERVIEW.
10. CONTROL CONVERSATIONS WITH QUESTIONS (TRUITT'S LAW).
11. NEVER ARGUE—AGREE AND THEN MAKE YOUR POINT.
12. ASK FOR REFERRALS—GET *SOMETHING* FROM EVERY CALL.
13. CONTROL YOUR ATTITUDE.
14. BE PERSISTENT.